EASTER BA~~KING AROUND~~ THE WORLD

Traditions, Stories, and

Irresistible Recipes

CONTENTS OF THE BOOK:

INTRODUCTION

Easter is a season of renewal, joy, and togetherness. Across the world, families gather to celebrate this special holiday with time-honored traditions, colorful decorations, and, of course, delicious baked goods that carry deep cultural significance. Whether it's the fragrant, braided Tsoureki of Greece, the fruit-filled Simnel Cake of England, or the airy, sweet Kulich of Ukraine, every country has its own way of honoring Easter through baking.

This book, "Easter Baking Around the World: Traditions, Stories, and Irresistible Recipes," is more than just a cookbook—it's a journey through the heart of global Easter traditions. You'll uncover the fascinating histories behind these beloved baked goods, from ancient customs that shaped their creation to the unique ingredients that give them their signature flavors.

But beyond history, this book is here to guide you in mastering these beautiful bakes in your own kitchen. Whether you're an experienced baker or just starting out, you'll find step-by-step instructions, expert tips, and baking secrets to ensure that every loaf, cake, and pastry turns out perfectly. You'll learn how to achieve the fluffiest dough, balance delicate spices, and create stunning, festive decorations that will impress family and friends.

Baking for Easter is not just about making food—

it's about creating memories. The scent of freshly baked bread filling the house, the joy of decorating a cake with loved ones, the excitement of breaking into a warm, golden loaf—these moments bring us closer together, just as they have for generations before us.

So, whether you're continuing a cherished family tradition or discovering a new Easter favorite, this book invites you to embrace the magic of Easter baking. Get ready to knead, shape, glaze, and bake your way through the most delightful recipes from around the world.

Let's begin this delicious journey—one Easter bake at a time!

CHAPTER 1:

The Sweet Tradition of Easter Baking

Easter, a celebration of renewal, joy, and hope, has long been associated with feasting and festivities. Central to these celebrations is the art of baking—an activity that brings families together and fills homes with the warm, inviting aroma of spices, fruits, and freshly baked dough. Easter baking is more than just a culinary tradition; it is a vibrant tapestry woven with history, culture, and faith.

A Celebration of Renewal and Abundance

Easter baking holds deep symbolic significance in many cultures. As the season coincides with spring in much of the world, it represents new beginnings, fertility, and the triumph of light over darkness. This is reflected in the rich ingredients used in Easter recipes, such as eggs, butter, sugar, and milk—symbols of abundance after the austerity of Lent.

For Christians, Easter is the culmination of Holy Week, marking the resurrection of Jesus Christ. Baking special breads and cakes for this occasion is a way to honor this sacred event. These baked goods often incorporate religious symbols, such as crosses, braids, and shapes that reflect the themes of life and resurrection.

Baking as a Universal Language

While Easter baking takes on unique forms across

the globe, its essence remains universal: it is an act of love, sharing, and celebration. From the rich, buttery Kulich of Ukraine to the delicate Colomba Pasquale of Italy, every region has its distinctive Easter recipes, each steeped in centuries-old traditions.

In Greece, Tsoureki—a sweet braided bread—captures the spirit of Easter with its rich flavors of mahleb and mastic, adorned with red-dyed eggs symbolizing the blood of Christ and new life. Meanwhile, in England, the hot cross bun is a hallmark of Good Friday, with its signature cross marking the crucifixion and spices symbolizing the embalming of Christ.

The Rituals of Easter Baking

Easter baking is often accompanied by cherished rituals, passed down through generations. Families gather in kitchens, kneading dough, mixing batter, and sharing stories of their ancestors. In many households, baking is not merely about the end product but the process—a time to bond, reflect, and create memories.

The act of baking also carries spiritual undertones in many cultures. In Poland, for example, families prepare intricate babkas and mazurkas, which are then blessed by priests during the Święconka (Easter basket blessing). Similarly, in parts of Latin America, special Easter breads and cakes are often shared with neighbors and the less fortunate, reinforcing community bonds.

Modern Twists on Timeless Traditions

While traditional Easter baking recipes remain popular, modern bakers often infuse them with contemporary twists. Vegan hot cross buns, gluten-free Simnel cakes, and chocolate-filled Tsourekis are just a few examples of how these time-honored recipes are being adapted for modern tastes and dietary needs.

Social media has also played a role in reviving and reinventing Easter baking traditions. Home bakers share their creations, from intricately decorated Easter egg cookies to towering layered cakes, inspiring others to embrace the joy of Easter baking.

A Journey Through Easter Baking

This chapter is just the beginning of our journey through the enchanting world of Easter baking. In the chapters that follow, we will explore Easter recipes from different cultures, uncover the stories behind them, and provide step-by-step guides to recreate these delights in your own kitchen. Whether you're baking for a family gathering, a community celebration, or simply to savor the joy of creation, Easter baking is a tradition that invites us all to connect with our roots, celebrate the present, and look forward to the future.

So, preheat your oven, gather your ingredients, and join us as we dive into the sweet and savory world of Easter baking traditions from around the globe. Let the journey begin!

CHAPTER 2:

Irresistible Easter Baking Recipes from Around the World

Easter baking is a culinary adventure that takes us through the heart of global traditions. Each recipe carries the flavors of its culture, the warmth of family gatherings, and the stories of generations.

This chapter is your passport to the most fascinating Easter treats from around the world.

1. HOT CROSS BUNS (ENGLAND)

History: Hot cross buns date back to 12th-century England, traditionally eaten on Good Friday. The cross atop these spiced buns symbolizes the crucifixion, while the spices represent the embalming of Christ.

INGREDIENTS:
4 cups all-purpose flour
1/4 cup sugar
2 1/4 tsp active dry yeast
1/2 tsp salt
1 tsp cinnamon
1/2 tsp nutmeg
1/2 cup raisins or currants
1 1/4 cups warm milk
4 tbsp unsalted butter, melted

1 egg, beaten
For the cross: 1/4 cup flour, 3 tbsp water
For the glaze: 2 tbsp apricot jam, warmed

INSTRUCTIONS:

- Mix flour, sugar, yeast, salt, cinnamon, nutmeg, and raisins in a bowl.
- Add warm milk, melted butter, and egg. Mix until a soft dough forms.
- Knead the dough for 8–10 minutes until smooth. Place in a greased bowl, cover, and let rise for 1 hour.
- Divide into 12 equal pieces. Shape into buns and place on a baking tray, leaving space for rising. Cover and let rise for 30 minutes.
- Mix flour and water for the cross. Pipe a cross onto each bun.
- Bake at 375°F (190°C) for 20 minutes or until golden brown.
- Brush with apricot jam glaze while warm.

Tips:
- Soak raisins in orange juice for extra flavor.
- Serve with butter or jam for a traditional touch.

2. TSOUREKI (GREECE)

History: This sweet braided bread is a staple in Greek Easter celebrations. Traditionally flavored with mahleb and mastic, it symbolizes the resurrection and new life. Red-dyed eggs are often baked into the dough, representing the blood of Christ.

INGREDIENTS:
4 1/2 cups bread flour
3/4 cup sugar
2 1/4 tsp active dry yeast
1/2 tsp salt
1/2 tsp mahleb (optional)
1/4 tsp ground mastic (optional)
1 cup warm milk
1/4 cup unsalted butter, melted

2 eggs, plus 1 egg for glazing
Red-dyed eggs (optional)

INSTRUCTIONS:
- Combine flour, sugar, yeast, salt, mahleb, and mastic in a large bowl.
- Add warm milk, melted butter, and eggs. Mix to form a dough.
- Knead for 8–10 minutes until smooth and elastic. Let rise for 2 hours in a warm place.
- Divide dough into three equal pieces. Roll each into a long strand and braid them. Place red-dyed eggs into the braid, if desired.
- Place the braid on a baking sheet, cover, and let rise for another hour.
- Brush with beaten egg and bake at 350°F (175°C) for 25–30 minutes.

Tips:
- Substitute mahleb and mastic with orange zest for a modern twist.
- Serve with a drizzle of honey for added sweetness.

3. COLOMBA PASQUALE (ITALY)

History: The Colomba Pasquale, or Easter Dove, is Italy's answer to the Christmas Panettone. Shaped like a dove to symbolize peace, this airy, fruit-studded bread is a quintessential Easter dessert.

INGREDIENTS:
3 cups all-purpose flour
1/2 cup sugar
2 1/4 tsp active dry yeast
1/2 cup warm milk
4 tbsp unsalted butter, softened
2 eggs
1/2 tsp vanilla extract
1/2 cup candied orange peel
1/4 cup almonds, for topping
For glaze: 1 egg white, 1/4 cup sugar

INSTRUCTIONS:

- Dissolve yeast in warm milk. Add a pinch of sugar and let activate for 5 minutes.
- In a bowl, combine flour, sugar, yeast mixture, butter, eggs, and vanilla. Knead into a soft dough.
- Incorporate candied orange peel and knead until evenly distributed. Let rise for 1 hour.
- Shape into a dove or loaf. Place on a baking tray, cover, and rise for 30 minutes.
- Brush with egg white, sprinkle sugar, and top with almonds.
- Bake at 350°F (175°C) for 40−45 minutes.

Tips:
- Use a Colomba mold for the traditional dove shape.
- Serve with coffee or dessert wine.

4. PASHKA (UKRAINE)

History: Pashka is a traditional Ukraine Easter dessert made from farmer's cheese (tvorog), sugar, and dried fruits. Shaped into a pyramid to symbolize the tomb of Christ, Pashka is often decorated with religious motifs, including the letters "XB," which stand for "Christ is Risen" in Cyrillic.

INGREDIENTS:
2 cups farmer's cheese or ricotta
1/2 cup unsalted butter, softened
1/2 cup sugar
1/2 cup heavy cream
1/4 cup chopped dried apricots
1/4 cup raisins
1/4 cup chopped almonds
1 tsp vanilla extract

INSTRUCTIONS:

- In a large bowl, beat the farmer's cheese, butter, and sugar until smooth.
- Gradually add heavy cream and vanilla extract, mixing until creamy.
- Stir in dried fruits and almonds.
- Line a Pashka mold or a fine sieve with cheesecloth. Spoon the mixture into the mold and press down firmly.
- Fold the cheesecloth over the top and place a weight on it. Refrigerate overnight to set.
- Unmold carefully onto a plate and decorate with dried fruits or nuts.

Tips:
- If you don't have a mold, use a flowerpot or a bowl with holes for drainage.
- Serve chilled with freshly baked kulich or on its own.

5. SIMNEL CAKE (UNITED KINGDOM)

History: This light fruitcake has been associated with Easter since medieval times. Its top layer of marzipan, adorned with 11 marzipan balls, symbolizes the apostles, excluding Judas. Traditionally, it was baked by daughters for their mothers on Mothering Sunday, a few weeks before Easter.

INGREDIENTS:
1 1/2 cups all-purpose flour
1 tsp baking powder
1/2 cup unsalted butter, softened
1/2 cup sugar
3 eggs
1/2 cup mixed dried fruits (currants, raisins, sultanas)

1/4 cup candied peel
1 tsp mixed spice
1/2 cup marzipan

INSTRUCTIONS:

- Preheat oven to 325°F (165°C). Grease and line an 8-inch round cake tin.
- Cream butter and sugar until light and fluffy. Add eggs one at a time, beating well.
- Fold in flour, baking powder, and mixed spice. Stir in dried fruits and peel.
- Spoon half the batter into the tin. Roll out marzipan into a circle and place on top. Add the remaining batter.
- Bake for 1 hour or until a skewer comes out clean. Cool completely.
- Roll out more marzipan to cover the cake. Create 11 marzipan balls for decoration.

Tips:
- Toast the marzipan under a broiler for a golden finish.
- Serve with tea for a quintessentially British experience.

6. KULICH (EASTERN EUROPE)

History: Kulich is a tall, cylindrical bread traditionally baked in Eastern Europe for Orthodox Easter. It's sweet, enriched with eggs and butter, and often flavored with vanilla or citrus zest. After baking, it's topped with sugar glaze and colorful sprinkles.

INGREDIENTS:
4 cups bread flour
1/2 cup sugar
1/4 cup butter, softened
1 cup warm milk
3 eggs
2 1/4 tsp active dry yeast
1/2 cup raisins
1 tsp vanilla extract

INSTRUCTIONS:

- Activate yeast in warm milk with a pinch of sugar. Let stand for 5 minutes.
- Combine flour, sugar, butter, eggs, and vanilla in a large bowl. Add yeast mixture and knead into a soft dough.
- Add raisins and knead until evenly distributed. Let rise for 2 hours.
- Shape dough and place in a tall, greased cylindrical tin or paper mold. Let rise for another hour.
- Bake at 350°F (175°C) for 30−35 minutes. Cool completely before glazing.
- For the glaze: Mix 1 cup powdered sugar with 2 tbsp milk. Drizzle over the kulich and decorate with sprinkles.

Tips:
- Use empty coffee cans as molds for an authentic shape.
- Pair with Pashka for a complete Easter spread.

7. EASTER LAMB COOKIES (FRANCE)

History: These lamb-shaped butter cookies symbolize the purity and innocence of the Lamb of God. Popular in Alsace, they are often dusted with powdered sugar or decorated with icing.

INGREDIENTS:
2 cups all-purpose flour
1/2 cup sugar
1/2 cup butter, chilled and cubed
1 egg
1 tsp vanilla extract

INSTRUCTIONS:
- In a bowl, mix flour and sugar. Add butter and rub into the flour until crumbly.
- Add egg and vanilla extract, mixing to form a

dough. Chill for 30 minutes.
- Roll out dough to 1/4 inch thick. Use lamb-shaped cookie cutters to cut out shapes.
- Place cookies on a baking sheet and bake at 350°F (175°C) for 10–12 minutes.
- Dust with powdered sugar or decorate with icing.

Tips:
- Add a pinch of cinnamon for a warm flavor.
- Serve with hot chocolate or coffee.

8. CAPIROTADA (MEXICO)

History: Capirotada is a traditional Mexican bread pudding made during Lent and Easter. It's a mix of bread, cheese, nuts, and dried fruits, with a syrup infused with cinnamon and cloves. Each ingredient symbolizes elements of the Passion of Christ.

INGREDIENTS:
6 slices of stale bread
1/4 cup grated cheese (e.g., panela or cheddar)
1/4 cup raisins
1/4 cup chopped pecans
2 cups water
1/2 cup piloncillo (or brown sugar)
1 cinnamon stick
2 cloves

INSTRUCTIONS:

- Toast bread slices until golden.
- In a saucepan, boil water with piloncillo, cinnamon, and cloves to create a syrup. Strain and set aside.
- In a baking dish, layer bread, cheese, raisins, and pecans. Pour syrup over each layer.
- Bake at 350°F (175°C) for 20 minutes. Serve warm.

Tips:

- Substitute piloncillo with honey for a lighter sweetness.
- Top with whipped cream for a modern twist.

9. CHOREG (CHOEREG) (ARMENIA)

History: Choreg is a sweet, buttery bread that graces Armenian Easter tables. Flavored with mahleb —a spice made from cherry seeds—this bread is braided and baked until golden, representing unity and renewal.

INGREDIENTS:
5 cups all-purpose flour
1 cup sugar
1 cup milk, warmed
2 1/4 tsp active dry yeast
1 cup unsalted butter, melted
3 eggs
1 tsp mahleb (optional)
1/2 tsp salt
Sesame seeds for topping

INSTRUCTIONS:

- Dissolve yeast in warm milk with a teaspoon of sugar. Let it activate for 5 minutes.
- In a large bowl, mix flour, sugar, mahleb, and salt.
- Add melted butter, eggs, and yeast mixture to the dry ingredients. Knead until smooth.
- Cover the dough and let rise for 2 hours.
- Divide dough into pieces, roll into ropes, and braid. Place on a baking sheet and let rise for 30 minutes.
- Brush with beaten egg and sprinkle with sesame seeds. Bake at 375°F (190°C) for 25–30 minutes.

Tips:
- Mahleb can be substituted with a mix of vanilla and almond extracts for a similar flavor.
- Serve warm with tea or coffee.

10. MÄMMI (FINLAND)

History: Mämmi is a Finnish Easter dessert made from rye flour, malt, and molasses. Traditionally prepared during Lent, it's baked slowly and served cold, often with cream or milk. Its earthy, sweet flavor reflects Finland's ancient culinary roots.

INGREDIENTS:
2 cups rye flour
1/2 cup malted rye powder
1/2 cup dark molasses
6 cups water
1/4 tsp salt
Zest of 1 orange (optional)

INSTRUCTIONS:

- Heat water in a large pot until warm, then gradually whisk in rye flour and malted rye powder.
- Add molasses, salt, and orange zest, stirring to combine.
- Pour the mixture into a greased, shallow baking dish. Cover with foil.
- Bake at 250°F (120°C) for 3–4 hours, stirring occasionally.
- Cool completely before refrigerating. Serve with cream or milk.

Tips:
- Mämmi improves in flavor after a day or two in the fridge.
- Add a drizzle of honey for a sweeter twist.

11. EASTER EGG BREAD (UNITED STATES)

History: A modern twist on traditional Italian Easter bread, this braided bread is baked with dyed eggs nestled in the dough. It's a centerpiece for Easter brunches in American homes, blending decoration and deliciousness.

INGREDIENTS:
4 cups bread flour
1/3 cup sugar
1 cup warm milk
2 1/4 tsp active dry yeast
2 eggs, plus 1 for glazing
1/4 cup unsalted butter, softened
1/2 tsp salt
6 dyed, uncooked eggs (optional)

INSTRUCTIONS:

- Dissolve yeast in warm milk with sugar. Let stand for 5 minutes.
- Combine flour and salt in a large bowl. Add yeast mixture, eggs, and butter. Knead into a soft dough.
- Let the dough rise for 1 hour.
- Divide the dough into three pieces, roll into ropes, and braid them. Tuck dyed eggs into the braid.
- Place on a baking sheet, brush with beaten egg, and bake at 350°F (175°C) for 25–30 minutes.

Tips:
- Use natural dyes (like beet juice or turmeric) for a rustic touch.
- Avoid eating the baked eggs if left out at room temperature for long.

12. OSTERFLADEN (SWITZERLAND)

History: Osterfladen, or "Easter tart," is a Swiss specialty. This almond and rice-based tart is sweet and creamy, with a pastry crust that balances its rich filling. It's a favorite in Swiss households during Easter.

INGREDIENTS:
For the crust:
1 1/2 cups all-purpose flour
1/4 cup sugar
1/2 cup butter, chilled and cubed
2–3 tbsp cold water
For the filling:
1/2 cup short-grain rice
2 cups milk
1/2 cup sugar

1/2 cup ground almonds
2 eggs, beaten
Zest of 1 lemon

INSTRUCTIONS:

- Prepare the crust by mixing flour and sugar. Cut in butter until crumbly, then add water to form a dough. Chill for 30 minutes.
- Roll out dough and line a tart pan. Pre-bake at 375°F (190°C) for 10 minutes.
- Cook rice in milk until soft. Cool slightly, then mix with sugar, almonds, eggs, and lemon zest.
- Pour filling into the crust and bake at 350°F (175°C) for 25–30 minutes.

Tips:
- Sprinkle powdered sugar on top for a festive touch.
- Serve with fresh berries for a refreshing contrast.

13. PINCA (CROATIA)

History: Pinca is a Croatian sweet bread made for Easter, characterized by its soft texture and slightly sweet, citrusy flavor. It's traditionally marked with a cross before baking, symbolizing the Crucifixion.

INGREDIENTS:
4 cups all-purpose flour
1/2 cup sugar
2 1/4 tsp active dry yeast
1/2 cup warm milk
1/4 cup unsalted butter, melted
3 eggs
Zest of 1 orange and 1 lemon
1 tsp vanilla extract

INSTRUCTIONS:
- Activate yeast in warm milk with a teaspoon of sugar. Let stand for 5 minutes.
- Mix flour, sugar, citrus zest, and yeast mixture. Add melted butter, eggs, and vanilla. Knead into a soft dough.
- Let rise for 2 hours. Shape into a round loaf, place on a baking sheet, and cut a cross on top.
- Brush with beaten egg and bake at 350°F (175°C) for 30–35 minutes.

Tips:
- Add a handful of raisins for extra texture.
- Serve warm with butter or jam.

14. BACALHAU BREAD (PORTUGAL)

History: Portugal is famous for its bacalhau (salt cod), and during Easter, this versatile fish finds its way into a savory bread. Bacalhau Bread is often served as an appetizer or as part of a festive meal. This hearty bread symbolizes the resourcefulness of Portuguese cuisine.

INGREDIENTS:
4 cups all-purpose flour
1 1/4 cups warm water
2 1/4 tsp active dry yeast
1 tsp sugar
1/4 cup olive oil
1 tsp salt
1 cup cooked, flaked salt cod
1/4 cup chopped fresh parsley
1/4 cup chopped black olives (optional)

INSTRUCTIONS:
- Dissolve yeast and sugar in warm water. Let sit for 5 minutes until frothy.
- In a large bowl, mix flour and salt. Add yeast mixture and olive oil, kneading until smooth.
- Fold in salt cod, parsley, and olives. Cover and let rise for 1 hour.
- Shape the dough into a loaf and place on a baking sheet. Let rise for another 30 minutes.
- Bake at 375°F (190°C) for 30–35 minutes until golden.

Tips:
- Soak salt cod in water overnight, changing the water several times, to remove excess salt.
- Serve with olive oil for dipping.

15. KOZUNAK (BULGARIA)

History: Kozunak is a traditional Bulgarian Easter bread, rich with eggs and sugar, symbolizing prosperity and joy. Often braided and topped with sugar or almonds, it's a festive centerpiece for the holiday table.

INGREDIENTS:
4 cups all-purpose flour
1/2 cup sugar
2 1/4 tsp active dry yeast
1/2 cup warm milk
1/4 cup unsalted butter, melted
3 eggs
Zest of 1 lemon
1/2 cup raisins (optional)
Slivered almonds for topping

INSTRUCTIONS:

- Dissolve yeast in warm milk with a teaspoon of sugar. Let stand for 5 minutes.
- Mix flour, sugar, and lemon zest in a large bowl. Add yeast mixture, eggs, and butter, kneading into a soft dough.
- Knead raisins into the dough (if using). Cover and let rise for 2 hours.
- Divide the dough into three pieces, braid them, and place on a baking sheet. Let rise for another hour.
- Brush with beaten egg, sprinkle with sugar and almonds, and bake at 350°F (175°C) for 30−35 minutes.

Tips:

- Serve with a dusting of powdered sugar for extra sweetness.
- Pair with a glass of warm milk or tea for a cozy treat.

16. PASTIERA NAPOLETANA (ITALY)

History: Pastiera is a Neapolitan Easter classic, blending ricotta, wheat berries, and candied citrus. This rich, creamy tart symbolizes renewal and abundance, with flavors reflecting Italy's spring harvest.

INGREDIENTS:
For the crust:
2 cups all-purpose flour
1/2 cup sugar
1/2 cup butter, chilled and cubed
1 egg
For the filling:
1/2 cup cooked wheat berries or farro
1 cup whole milk

1/2 cup sugar
1 cup ricotta cheese
3 eggs
Zest of 1 orange and 1 lemon
1/4 cup candied citrus peel

INSTRUCTIONS:

- Prepare the crust by mixing flour, sugar, and butter. Add the egg and knead into a dough. Chill for 30 minutes.
- Simmer wheat berries in milk and sugar until tender. Cool and mix with ricotta, eggs, citrus zest, and peel.
- Roll out the crust and line a tart pan. Pour in the filling.
- Bake at 350°F (175°C) for 50–60 minutes until set. Cool before serving.

Tips:
- Allow the tart to rest overnight for flavors to develop fully.
- Serve with a dollop of whipped cream.

17. MAZANEC (CZECH REPUBLIC)

History: Mazanec is a sweet bread traditionally baked in the Czech Republic for Easter. Enriched with eggs and butter, it's often flavored with raisins and almonds. The bread's round shape symbolizes the sun and the renewal of life.

INGREDIENTS:
4 cups all-purpose flour
1/2 cup sugar
2 1/4 tsp active dry yeast
1 cup warm milk
1/4 cup unsalted butter, melted
2 eggs
1/2 cup raisins
Slivered almonds for topping

INSTRUCTIONS:

- Activate yeast in warm milk with a teaspoon of sugar. Let sit for 5 minutes.
- Mix flour, sugar, and raisins in a bowl. Add yeast mixture, eggs, and butter. Knead until smooth.
- Let the dough rise for 1 hour. Shape into a round loaf and place on a baking sheet. Let rise again for 30 minutes.
- Brush with beaten egg, sprinkle with almonds, and bake at 350°F (175°C) for 30−35 minutes.

Tips:
- Serve warm with butter or honey.
- Add orange zest for a fresh, citrusy flavor.

18. KAHK (EGYPT)

History: Kahk, Egyptian buttery cookies filled with dates, nuts, or honey, date back to ancient times. They're a staple of festive celebrations, including Easter, symbolizing joy and hospitality.

INGREDIENTS:
2 cups all-purpose flour
1/2 cup ghee or unsalted butter, melted
1/4 cup powdered sugar
1/2 tsp baking powder
1/2 tsp ground cinnamon
1/4 cup milk
Date paste or chopped nuts for filling

INSTRUCTIONS:

- Mix flour, baking powder, sugar, and cinnamon. Add melted ghee and rub into the flour until crumbly.
- Gradually add milk to form a soft dough. Chill for 15 minutes.
- Take a small piece of dough, flatten it, and place a small amount of filling in the center. Roll into a ball.
- Press with a decorative mold or leave plain.
- Bake at 350°F (175°C) for 12−15 minutes until golden.

Tips:
- Dust with powdered sugar before serving.
- Store in an airtight container to maintain freshness.

19. BABOVKA (CZECH REPUBLIC)

History: Babovka is a traditional Czech Easter bundt cake made with yeast or baking powder, often flavored with vanilla, rum, or cocoa. Its circular shape symbolizes unity and eternity, making it a staple of Easter festivities.

INGREDIENTS:
3 cups all-purpose flour
1 cup sugar
1 cup milk
1/2 cup unsalted butter, melted
3 eggs
2 tsp baking powder
1 tsp vanilla extract
2 tbsp cocoa powder

INSTRUCTIONS:

- Preheat oven to 350°F (175°C). Grease and flour a bundt pan.
- Beat eggs and sugar until fluffy. Add melted butter, milk, and vanilla.
- Mix flour and baking powder, then gradually fold into the wet ingredients.
- Pour half the batter into the bundt pan. Mix cocoa powder into the remaining batter and pour over the top. Swirl with a knife for a marbled effect.
- Bake for 40–45 minutes. Cool completely before removing from the pan.

Tips:
- Dust with powdered sugar or drizzle with chocolate glaze for decoration.
- Serve with fresh fruit or whipped cream.

20. EASTER BUNNY ROLLS (UNITED STATES)

History: Easter Bunny Rolls are whimsical, bunny-shaped bread rolls popular in the United States. These rolls are fun for kids and adults alike, adding a playful touch to the Easter table.

INGREDIENTS:
3 cups bread flour
1/4 cup sugar
1 cup warm milk
2 1/4 tsp active dry yeast
1/4 cup unsalted butter, melted
1 egg
Pinch of salt

INSTRUCTIONS:

- Dissolve yeast in warm milk with a teaspoon of sugar. Let stand for 5 minutes.
- Mix flour, sugar, and salt in a bowl. Add yeast mixture, egg, and butter, kneading until smooth.
- Cover and let the dough rise for 1 hour.
- Divide dough into pieces and shape into bunny heads, ears, and tails. Place on a baking sheet and let rise for 30 minutes.
- Bake at 350°F (175°C) for 15–20 minutes until golden.

Tips:
- Use raisins or chocolate chips for bunny eyes.
- Serve warm with butter or jam for a delightful treat.

21. EASTER PRETZELS (GERMANY)

History: Easter pretzels have a long history in Germany, where pretzels are believed to symbolize arms folded in prayer. These soft, salty treats are enjoyed during Lent and Easter.

INGREDIENTS:
3 cups all-purpose flour
1 tsp sugar
1 1/4 cups warm water
2 1/4 tsp active dry yeast
1/4 cup unsalted butter, melted
1 tsp salt
1/4 cup baking soda
Coarse salt for topping

INSTRUCTIONS:

- Dissolve yeast and sugar in warm water. Let sit for 5 minutes.
- Mix flour and salt in a bowl. Add yeast mixture and melted butter, kneading into a smooth dough.
- Let rise for 1 hour. Divide dough into pieces, roll into ropes, and shape into pretzels.
- Boil water with baking soda and dip each pretzel into the solution for 30 seconds.
- Place pretzels on a baking sheet, sprinkle with coarse salt, and bake at 400°F (200°C) for 12–15 minutes until golden.

Tips:
- Serve warm with mustard or melted cheese for dipping.
- Add a touch of cinnamon sugar for a sweet version.

22. SEMLA BUNS (SWEDEN)

History: Semla buns, traditionally enjoyed before Lent, have become an Easter favorite in Sweden. These cardamom-scented buns are filled with almond paste and whipped cream, offering a luxurious taste of spring.

INGREDIENTS:
4 cups all-purpose flour
1/2 cup sugar
2 1/4 tsp active dry yeast
1 cup warm milk
1/4 cup unsalted butter, melted
1 egg
1 tsp ground cardamom
For the filling:
1/2 cup almond paste
1/2 cup whipped cream

INSTRUCTIONS:

- Activate yeast in warm milk with a teaspoon of sugar. Let sit for 5 minutes.
- Mix flour, sugar, and cardamom in a bowl. Add yeast mixture, butter, and egg. Knead into a soft dough.
- Cover and let rise for 1 hour. Shape into small buns and place on a baking sheet. Let rise again for 30 minutes.
- Bake at 350°F (175°C) for 15−20 minutes until golden. Cool completely.
- Hollow out the buns, fill with almond paste, and top with whipped cream. Place the bun tops back on and dust with powdered sugar.

Tips:

- For a nut-free version, substitute almond paste with vanilla custard.
- Chill the buns before serving for a refreshing treat.

23. ROSCA DE PASCUA (ARGENTINA)

History: Rosca de Pascua is a traditional Argentine Easter bread, often adorned with pastry cream, dried fruits, and colorful sprinkles. Its circular shape symbolizes eternal life and unity, making it a centerpiece for Easter festivities.

INGREDIENTS:
4 cups all-purpose flour
1/2 cup sugar
2 1/4 tsp active dry yeast
1/2 cup warm milk
1/4 cup unsalted butter, melted
3 eggs
1 tsp vanilla extract
Zest of 1 lemon

For decoration:
1 cup pastry cream
Candied cherries, raisins, and sprinkles

INSTRUCTIONS:

- Activate yeast in warm milk with a teaspoon of sugar. Let sit for 5 minutes.
- Mix flour, sugar, and lemon zest in a bowl. Add yeast mixture, eggs, butter, and vanilla, kneading until smooth.
- Let dough rise for 1–2 hours until doubled in size.
- Shape dough into a ring, place on a baking sheet, and let rise again for 1 hour.
- Pipe pastry cream decoratively on top and add candied cherries or raisins.
- Bake at 350°F (175°C) for 25–30 minutes. Once cooled, sprinkle with colorful sprinkles.

Tips:

- Substitute pastry cream with dulce de leche for a richer flavor.
- Serve with a cup of yerba mate for an authentic pairing.

24. MAZUREK (POLAND)

History: Mazurek is a Polish Easter pastry, known for its shortbread-like crust and rich toppings of caramel, chocolate, or fruit preserves. It's decorated with nuts, dried fruits, and intricate patterns, embodying the joy of Easter.

INGREDIENTS:
For the crust:
2 cups all-purpose flour
1/2 cup sugar
1/2 cup unsalted butter, chilled and cubed
2 egg yolks
2 tbsp cold water
For the topping:
1/2 cup caramel or chocolate spread
Assorted nuts and dried fruits

INSTRUCTIONS:

- Preheat oven to 350°F (175°C). Grease a tart pan.
- Mix flour and sugar. Cut in butter until crumbly. Add egg yolks and water, mixing into a dough.
- Press dough into the tart pan and bake for 20−25 minutes until golden. Cool completely.
- Spread caramel or chocolate on the crust. Decorate with nuts and dried fruits.

Tips:
- Use a mix of almonds, walnuts, and apricots for varied textures.
- Drizzle with white chocolate for an elegant finish.

25. PAN DE PASCUA (CHILE)

History: Pan de Pascua, a spiced fruitcake, is traditionally enjoyed in Chile during Easter and Christmas. It combines European baking techniques with local flavors like rum and cinnamon.

INGREDIENTS:
2 cups all-purpose flour
1 tsp baking powder
1/2 tsp ground cinnamon
1/4 tsp ground cloves
1/4 tsp nutmeg
1/2 cup unsalted butter, softened
1 cup sugar
2 eggs
1/4 cup rum
1/2 cup raisins
1/2 cup chopped walnuts

INSTRUCTIONS:

- Preheat oven to 350°F (175°C). Grease a loaf pan.
- Mix flour, baking powder, cinnamon, cloves, and nutmeg.
- Cream butter and sugar until fluffy. Add eggs one at a time, then mix in rum.
- Gradually add dry ingredients, folding in raisins and walnuts.
- Pour batter into the loaf pan and bake for 50–60 minutes.

Tips:
- Soak raisins in rum overnight for enhanced flavor.
- Serve with a cup of spiced tea for a cozy pairing.

26. KRANTZ CAKE (CHOCOLATE BABKA) – ISRAEL

History: Krantz Cake, also known as Chocolate Babka, is a rich, twisted yeast cake of Jewish origin. Though often assoicated with Jewish bakeries worldwide, it has become an Easter treat in Israel. The braided shape represents unity, while the rich chocolate filling adds festive indulgence.

INGREDIENTS:
4 cups all-purpose flour
1/4 cup sugar
2 1/4 tsp active dry yeast
1/2 cup warm milk
2 eggs
1/2 cup unsalted butter, softened
1/2 tsp salt

For the filling:
1/2 cup unsalted butter, melted
1 cup dark chocolate, finely chopped
1/4 cup cocoa powder
1/2 cup sugar

For the syrup:
1/2 cup water
1/2 cup sugar

INSTRUCTIONS:

- Activate yeast in warm milk with a teaspoon of sugar. Let sit for 5 minutes.
- In a large bowl, mix flour, sugar, and salt. Add yeast mixture, eggs, and butter. Knead until smooth. Let rise for 1.5 hours.
- Roll out dough into a rectangle. Spread melted butter, then sprinkle chocolate, cocoa, and sugar.
- Roll into a log, slice lengthwise, and twist the two halves together. Place in a greased loaf pan. Let rise for another hour.
- Bake at 350°F (175°C) for 30−35 minutes.
- Make the syrup by heating sugar and water until dissolved. Brush over the hot babka.

Tips:
- Use Nutella instead of chocolate for an easier version.
- Toast slices and serve with coffee for a perfect Easter breakfast.

27. SAFFRON BUNS (PÅSKBULLAR) – SWEDEN

History: Saffron Buns, or Påskbullar, are a Swedish Easter treat similar to St. Lucia buns but are specifically made for Easter with a light, buttery texture and a golden hue from saffron.

INGREDIENTS:
4 cups all-purpose flour
1/2 cup sugar
2 1/4 tsp active dry yeast
1/2 cup warm milk
1/4 tsp saffron threads, crushed
1/4 cup unsalted butter, melted
1 egg
1/2 cup raisins

INSTRUCTIONS:

- Soak saffron in warm milk for 5 minutes.
- In a large bowl, mix flour, sugar, and yeast. Add saffron milk, butter, and egg. Knead into a dough.
- Let rise for 1.5 hours.
- Shape into small rolls, place on a baking sheet, and let rise again for 30 minutes.
- Brush with egg wash and bake at 350°F (175°C) for 15–20 minutes.

Tips:
- Serve with warm milk for a traditional Swedish touch.
- Add cardamom for extra spice.

28. LAMB-SHAPED CAKE (BARANEK WIELKANOCNY) – POLAND

History: In Poland, a lamb-shaped cake symbolizes Jesus as the "Lamb of God." Traditionally made from a light sponge cake, it is often the centerpiece of the Easter table.

INGREDIENTS:
1 1/2 cups all-purpose flour
1 cup sugar
1/2 cup unsalted butter, softened
4 eggs
1/4 cup milk
1 tsp vanilla extract
1 tsp baking powder

INSTRUCTIONS:

- Preheat oven to 350°F (175°C). Grease a lamb-shaped cake mold.
- Beat butter and sugar until fluffy. Add eggs one at a time.
- Mix flour and baking powder, then add to the batter along with milk and vanilla.
- Pour into the mold and bake for 35–40 minutes.
- Cool completely before removing from the mold. Dust with powdered sugar.

Tips:
- Use chocolate frosting for a richer version.
- Tie a red ribbon around the lamb's neck for a festive presentation.

29. VÁNOČKA (EASTER BRAIDED BREAD) – CZECH REPUBLIC & SLOVAKIA

History: Vánočka is a rich, buttery braided bread similar to challah but infused with almonds and raisins. Though it is commonly eaten at Christmas, it also holds significance in Easter celebrations as a symbol of prosperity.

INGREDIENTS:
4 cups all-purpose flour
1/2 cup sugar
2 1/4 tsp active dry yeast
1 cup warm milk
2 eggs
1/2 cup butter, melted
1 tsp vanilla extract
1/2 cup raisins
1/2 cup sliced almonds
1 egg yolk + 1 tbsp water (for egg wash)

INSTRUCTIONS:
- Dissolve yeast in warm milk with a teaspoon of sugar. Let sit for 5 minutes.
- In a large bowl, mix flour, sugar, and yeast mixture. Add eggs, melted butter, and vanilla. Knead until smooth. Let rise for 2 hours.
- Fold in raisins and divide into three sections. Braid the dough and let rise for another hour.
- Brush with egg wash, sprinkle with almonds, and bake at 350°F (175°C) for 30–35 minutes.

30. PÃO DE DEUS (BREAD OF GOD) – PORTUGAL

History: Pão de Deus, meaning "Bread of God," is a sweet coconut-topped bun traditionally enjoyed on Easter and religious holidays in Portugal. It has a soft, pillowy texture and a delicious coconut crust.

INGREDIENTS:
3 1/2 cups all-purpose flour
1/2 cup sugar
2 1/4 tsp active dry yeast
1/2 cup warm milk
2 eggs
1/4 cup butter, melted
Zest of 1 lemon
1/2 tsp salt

For topping:
1/2 cup shredded coconut
1/4 cup sugar
1 egg yolk
2 tbsp milk

INSTRUCTIONS:

- Dissolve yeast in warm milk with 1 tsp sugar. Let sit for 5 minutes.
- In a large bowl, mix flour, sugar, lemon zest, and salt. Add eggs, butter, and yeast mixture. Knead into a soft dough. Let rise for 2 hours.
- Shape into small buns and place on a baking sheet. Let rise for another hour.
- Mix shredded coconut, sugar, egg yolk, and milk for the topping. Spread over buns.
- Bake at 350°F (175°C) for 20−25 minutes.

Tips:
- Best served warm with butter.
- Try adding a hint of vanilla extract to the dough for extra flavor.

CHAPTER 3:

Baking Secrets & Expert Tips

Master the Art of Perfect Dough, Achieve the Ideal Rise, and Enhance Flavors with Traditional Techniques from Expert Bakers

Easter baking is as much about tradition and symbolism as it is about technique. The perfect loaf of Tsoureki, the airy texture of Hot Cross Buns, or the rich crumb of Pastiera Napoletana all require skill, patience, and a few expert secrets. Whether you're a seasoned baker or new to the craft, mastering these techniques will ensure that your Easter treats turn out flawless every time.

In this chapter, we will explore:

■ The science of dough and how to achieve the perfect texture

■ Secrets to a high and even rise

■ Enhancing flavors with traditional techniques

■ Troubleshooting common baking problems

■ Storage and serving tips to keep your Easter bakes fresh and delicious

Let's dive in!

1. The Science of Dough: Achieving the Perfect Texture

Dough is the foundation of most Easter bakes, from soft breads to flaky pastries. Understanding how ingredients interact will help you achieve the ideal texture and consistency.

A. The Role of Key Ingredients
Each ingredient in a dough recipe serves a purpose:
- Flour – The structure builder. Different flours yield different textures:
- All-purpose flour: Versatile for most Easter breads.
- Bread flour: High in protein, giving structure to enriched doughs.
- Cake flour: Low in protein, perfect for delicate pastries.

Yeast – The magic behind rising dough. Choose the right type:
- Active dry yeast: Needs proofing in warm liquid before use.
- Instant yeast: Can be mixed directly into dry ingredients.
- Fresh yeast: Used in traditional recipes for a more complex flavor.

Sugar – Not just for sweetness! Sugar also feeds yeast, tenderizes dough, and adds golden color.

Eggs – Enrich the dough, adding flavor, tenderness, and a beautiful golden hue.

Fats (Butter, Oil, or Lard) – Help create a soft, rich crumb. Butter adds a deep, luxurious flavor.

Liquid (Milk, Water, or Juice) – Hydrates flour, activating gluten. Warm liquids (not too hot!) help yeast thrive.

Salt – Balances sweetness and strengthens gluten structure.

B. Kneading: Why It Matters

Kneading develops gluten, which gives dough structure and elasticity. Here's how to tell if you've kneaded enough:

The windowpane test: Stretch a small piece of dough between your fingers. If it forms a thin, translucent sheet without tearing, it's ready.

Dough should feel smooth, slightly tacky but not sticky.

💡 Tip: Avoid over-kneading enriched doughs (with eggs, butter, or milk), as it can break down gluten and make the dough too soft.

2. Secrets to a High and Even Rise

A. The Perfect Proofing Environment

Proofing (rising) is essential for light and fluffy baked goods. Here's how to get it right:

■ Warmth is key: Ideal proofing temperature is 75–85°F (24–29°C). A slightly warm oven (turned off) or a proofing box works well.

■ Humidity matters: If your kitchen is dry, place a bowl of warm water in the oven with the dough to prevent drying out.

■ Be patient: Rushing proofing can result in dense,

underdeveloped flavors. Let the dough rise until it doubles in size.

B. *How to Tell When Dough is Fully Proofed*
Poke test: Gently press a finger into the dough.
- If the indentation springs back slowly, it's ready to bake.
- If it bounces back immediately, it needs more time.
- If it deflates, it has over-proofed and may result in a collapsed bake.

❢ Tip: Enriched doughs (like Kulich or Tsoureki) rise slower due to fats and eggs. Give them extra time!

3. *Enhancing Flavors with Traditional Techniques*
A. *Fermentation for Better Flavor*
For deeper, more complex flavors, try cold fermentation:

Let dough rise overnight in the fridge. This slows yeast activity, developing rich flavors.

Works well for Hot Cross Buns, Kulich, and Brioche-style Easter breads.

B. *Traditional Spices & Flavorings*
Many Easter bakes feature signature flavors passed down for generations:
- Citrus zest (lemon, orange) – Adds brightness.
- Mahleb (Greek baking spice) – A key ingredient in Tsoureki, giving it a unique cherry-almond aroma.

69

- Rosewater or Orange Blossom Water – Used in Middle Eastern and Mediterranean Easter pastries.
- Anise & Cardamom – Common in Italian and Scandinavian Easter breads.

💡 Tip: Toasting spices before adding them intensifies their flavors!

4. Troubleshooting Common Baking Problems

■ Dense or Heavy Bread?
- Dough was under-kneaded or under-proofed.
- Too much flour—always measure carefully!

■ Dough Didn't Rise?
- Yeast may be old or killed by too-hot liquid.
- Room was too cold—try a warm oven for proofing.

■ Cracked or Dry Pastry?
- Not enough moisture—cover dough while resting.
- Overbaked—check your oven temperature with an oven thermometer.

■ Soggy Bottom?
- Bake on a preheated baking stone or a metal sheet for better heat distribution.
- Let baked goods cool on a wire rack to prevent trapped steam.

5. Storage & Serving Tips for Easter Bakes

A. Keeping Breads Fresh

Wrap in a clean kitchen towel to keep moisture in.

For longer storage, freeze in an airtight bag (up to 3 months).

B. Reviving Stale Breads
Warm slightly in the oven at 300°F (150°C) for 10 minutes.

Steam method: Place in a microwave with a cup of water for 30 seconds.

C. Serving Ideas
Kulich pairs beautifully with Paskha (Russian Easter cheese dessert).

Hot Cross Buns are best toasted with butter or jam.

Easter Babka can be transformed into French toast the next day.

Final Thoughts
Baking for Easter is more than just making delicious treats—it's about preserving traditions, bringing families together, and celebrating renewal. By mastering the techniques in this chapter, you'll be able to bake with confidence, ensuring every Easter table is filled with warmth, love, and irresistible flavors. ●✦

HERE YOU CAN POST YOUR EASTER BAKING RECIPES

Recipe:

Rating: ☆☆☆☆☆ Difficulty: ☆☆☆☆☆ Prep Time: Cook Time:

Ingredients:

Cooking Instructions:

Thoughts and Notes:

Recipe:

Rating: ☆☆☆☆☆ Difficulty: ☆☆☆☆☆ Prep Time: Cook Time:

Ingredients:

Cooking Instructions:

Thoughts and Notes:

Recipe:

Rating: ☆☆☆☆☆ Difficulty: ☆☆☆☆☆ Prep Time: Cook Time:

Ingredients:

_____

_____

_____

_____

_____

_____

Cooking Instructions:

_____

_____

_____

_____

_____

_____

_____

_____

_____

_____

Thoughts and Notes:

_____

_____

_____

_____

_____

Recipe:

Rating: ☆☆☆☆☆ Difficulty: ☆☆☆☆☆ Prep Time: Cook Time:

Ingredients:

_____

_____

_____

_____

_____

Cooking Instructions:

_____

_____

_____

_____

_____

_____

_____

_____

_____

Thoughts and Notes:

_____

_____

_____

_____

_____

Recipe:

Rating: ☆☆☆☆☆ Difficulty: ☆☆☆☆☆ Prep Time: Cook Time:

Ingredients:

Cooking Instructions:

Thoughts and Notes:

Recipe:

Rating: ☆☆☆☆☆ Difficulty: ☆☆☆☆☆ Prep Time: Cook Time:

Ingredients:

Cooking Instructions:

Thoughts and Notes:

Recipe:

Rating: ☆☆☆☆☆ Difficulty: ☆☆☆☆☆ Prep Time: Cook Time:

Ingredients:

Cooking Instructions:

Thoughts and Notes:

Recipe:

Rating: ☆☆☆☆☆ Difficulty: ☆☆☆☆☆ Prep Time: _____ Cook Time: _____

Ingredients:

Cooking Instructions:

Thoughts and Notes:

Recipe:

Rating: ☆☆☆☆☆ Difficulty: ☆☆☆☆☆ Prep Time: Cook Time:

Ingredients:

Cooking Instructions:

Thoughts and Notes:

Recipe:

Rating: ☆☆☆☆☆ Difficulty: ☆☆☆☆☆ Prep Time: Cook Time:

Ingredients:

Cooking Instructions:

Thoughts and Notes:

Recipe:

Rating: ☆☆☆☆☆ Difficulty: ☆☆☆☆☆ Prep Time: Cook Time:

Ingredients:

Cooking Instructions:

Thoughts and Notes:

Recipe:

Rating: ☆☆☆☆☆ Difficulty: ☆☆☆☆☆ Prep Time: Cook Time:

Ingredients:

Cooking Instructions:

Thoughts and Notes:

Recipe:

Rating: ☆☆☆☆☆ Difficulty: ☆☆☆☆☆ Prep Time: Cook Time:

Ingredients:

Cooking Instructions:

Thoughts and Notes:

Recipe:

Rating: ☆☆☆☆☆ Difficulty: ☆☆☆☆☆ Prep Time: Cook Time:

Ingredients:

Cooking Instructions:

Thoughts and Notes:

Recipe:

Rating: ☆☆☆☆☆ Difficulty: ☆☆☆☆☆ Prep Time: Cook Time:

Ingredients:

Cooking Instructions:

Thoughts and Notes:

Made in the USA
Monee, IL
29 March 2025

14840961R00057